The WORKBASKET
Sewing
Workbook

PLANNING,
TIPS AND IDEAS
for the
PASSIONATE
SEWIST

Edited by Bethany Anderson

KRAUSE PUBLICATIONS
CINCINNATI, OHIO

THIS BOOK BELONGS TO

_____

_____

_____

Why The WORKBASKET

At their kitchen table in October 1935, Clara Tillotson and her husband John created the first eight-page service bulletin that eventually turned into *The WORKBASKET* magazine, which inspired readers for sixty-one years. It was the go-to for *"IDEAS for the Bazaar, the Home, Gifts and Sparetime Money-makers—with Many Inexpensive, Easily Made Articles that find a Ready Sale,"* with endless projects and suggestions in knitting, crochet, quilting, embroidery and many other fun crafts.

The content pulled for your workbook is from the 1940s, '50s and '60s. During that time there was a rebirth in sewing and being proud to sew, especially your own clothes. Many readers of *The WORKBASKET* who, decades ago, inspired one another to add more to their pin money can still inspire and offer tips for today's passionate sewist.

They Sew For Fun

"Because they enjoy it" was recently given by more women who sew as the reason for making their own clothes than any of the many other reasons. We might add individual styling and certainly the saving of money; both are highly important reasons for making one's wardrobe, but these came second and third in a survey that was recently called to our attention.

To those who have never known the thrill of choosing fabric and pattern, as well as the developing of a costume to their very own liking and fit, we recommend sewing. Fashioning one's clothing is not only a very wise use of time and money, it brings unending and thrilling satisfaction as well, and offers a challenge to the artistic ability of every woman and girl who tries it.

With higher taxes and price increases in many commodities limiting the purchasing power of the average income, the family's clothing allowance will probably be the first to be cut. It is positively astounding how far the clothing dollar can be stretched by the women who sew. We are told there are over twenty-eight million women and girls now actively saving by sewing; or we might say, they have more clothes because they do sew. This number could easily be doubled by the many non-sewers who can become interested by the unlimited possibilities that sewing holds for them.

The larger magazines for women, daily papers, and pattern and fabric manufacturers are all aware of this new interest and are making more available to all who sew or want to learn the best in fashion. There are many helpful books in the libraries and bookstores; the many pattern companies offer inspiring pamphlets; and the manufacturers of sewing machines offer courses of instruction.

So if you want to help stretch the ever-shrinking household dollar, join the millions of women and girls who this year, because of home sewing, will be smartly attired in becoming garments that they can pridefully display as the product of their own industry and ingenuity.

April 1951 issue of *The WORKBASKET*

Checkpoints in Fitting

Place garment on the figure or dress form and pin the center front and center back in position so the lengthwise grain is perpendicular to the floor. The hip seams should come directly over the hip bones and also fall perpendicular to the floor. Then check the crosswise grainlines at the bust, waist and hip to be sure these lines are parallel with the floor.

1. First check the neckline for comfort.

2. Check the shoulder line for position and correct length.

3. Check the sleeve for the grainline and the armhole for position and appearance.

4. Check the fit across the bust and underarm seams for comfort and smoothness.

5. Make sure that the waistline is in the proper position and is fitted with ease.

6. The hipline should not fit tightly. The skirt should swing freely from this line.

7. Don't forget to ensure enough ease under the hipline for movement.

8. Make sure that the length and width of the sleeve is adequate and that the cuffs are in proportion to the hand size.

9. Finally, mark the hem at the proper width for the style and fabric.

As you are fitting the garment, keep the overall appearance in mind, too. Proportion is important. Is the collar too wide or bulky? Are the lapels too wide? Are the pockets too big? Would they look better placed higher or lower? Are the sleeves too wide, too long, too full? Check the belt. Should it be made of leather? Is it too wide or narrow? Does it cover the waistline seam adequately? What about buttons? Would larger or smaller ones look better? Do not hesitate to make these changes if they will improve your appearance.

February 1964

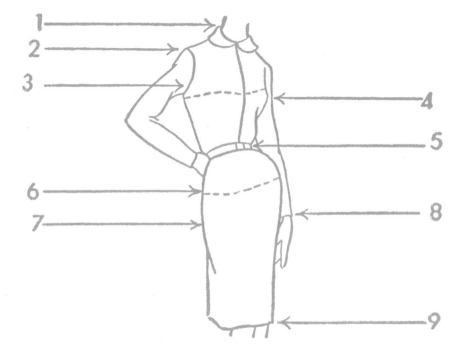

Project Checklist

Project name: _____

Date started: _____

Project description: _____

_____

Occasion/use: _____

Measurements: _____

_____

_____

_____

_____

Fabrics: _____

_____

_____

Thread type: _____

Interfacing type: _____

Needle type: _____

Special notions needed: _____

_____

_____

Needlework Advisor

Recently it became necessary for me to augment our income, what with sickness over a long period of time and all. There was nothing I could do, I thought, since I am confined most of the time to a wheelchair. But my niece came in one day to ask for advice about making over a blouse and asked me why I didn't make use of my skill in that direction. I reminded her that I had never cared for sewing, but she said she didn't mean actually sewing. She herself was there to find out how to do something relatively simple, and there must be dozens of other women, too, who needed such help. So two afternoons a week, at first, I had friends, neighbors and their friends come to the house with their sewing and "makeover" problems—fitting, repairing, lengthening, shortening, skirts, sleeves, all of those things that are so arduous if you don't know how. It has been wonderful for me. I use my own sewing machine, a borrowed portable, and one of the women who comes most often brings her small table sewing machine, and I now have "classes" four afternoons, one morning and two evenings every week. I charge each person $1 for attending one class each week, $1.50 if they attend two, $2 if they come to three. While I'm making a good little amount for myself and my family needs, I'm also teaching women a whole lot about simple sewing. I've found that there are women, lots of them, who don't know how to pull bastings, fell a seam, sew on snaps or even press, and many had never known how to use a paper pattern. I like what I am doing, and I myself often don't have to sew a stitch!

— *Lucy Schurmer Lenden*

From "Women Who Make Cents"
April 1955 issue of *The* **WORKBASKET**

My Design

Title: _____

Date started: _____

Project description: _____

_____

Occasion/use: _____

Measurements: _____

_____

Fabrics: _____

_____

_____

Notions: _____

Special notes: _____

_____

Changes to original concept: _____

_____

_____

Date completed: _____

fabric

DATE: _____

SOURCE: _____

YARDAGE: _____

COST: _____

DATE: _____

SOURCE: _____

YARDAGE: _____

COST: _____

DATE: _____

SOURCE: _____

YARDAGE: _____

COST: _____

DATE: _____

SOURCE: _____

YARDAGE: _____

COST: _____

DATE: _____

SOURCE: _____

YARDAGE: _____

COST: _____

DATE: _____

SOURCE: _____

YARDAGE: _____

COST: _____

DATE: _____

SOURCE: _____

YARDAGE: _____

COST: _____

DATE: _____

SOURCE: _____

YARDAGE: _____

COST: _____

Gifts IN A *Jiff*

DATE MADE/NEEDED: . . . .

OCCASION:. . . . .

FOR WHOM: . . . .

PROJECT DESCRIPTION: . . . .

. . . .

MATERIALS: . . . .

. . . .

COST PER GIFT: . . . .

Salvaged Sewing Kits

Empty lipstick cases make convenient sewing kits for the handbag. I wash the cases in warm suds, then rinse and dry them thoroughly. Next I press a small wad of cotton into the bottom and stick three needles, threaded with black, white and tan thread, into the cotton. Two or three buttons and safety pins may be added. I sell all I can make for $1 each.

— Hilda Smith

From "Women Who Make Cents"
January 1950 issue of *The WORKBASKET*

Triumphs

	COMPLETED DATE
1.	
2.	
3.	
4.	
5.	

. . . .

Conquer

	GOAL DATE
1.	
2.	
3.	
4.	
5.	

FIGURE VARIATIONS
CREATE NEED FOR ALTERATIONS

On the facing page are some illustrated tips that professional dress-makers use to make slight alterations:

✳ Rounded Shoulders—If the back of the armhole appears too full and causes ripples, use a small dart at the center of each shoulder, tapering down the back. Space evenly from the center of the neck and shoulder seams.

✳ Flat Chest—Raise the front shoulder seam at the neck to take up any sag in the front of the blouse. Reshape the neckline by marking the reshaping with tailor's chalk, then cut along chalk line.

✳ Rounded Tummy—If the tummy has a rounded look, special fitting is necessary or the center front hemline of the skirt will stand out; this can be altered by taking up the sides of the skirt at the waistline.

✳ Full Bust—More length is needed in the front bodice pieces than at the back. Allow extra length in cutting. Fit the extra fullness at the side by taking a dart under the arm and narrowing it toward the bust.

✳ Sway Back—A sway back can be worked out of, but a curve in the wrong place will cause a wrinkle across the back below the waistline. Lift the skirt at the center, and fit the extra fold into the waistline seam at the back.

June 1951

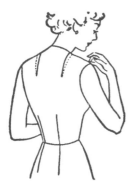

Rounded Shoulders   Flat Chest   Rounded Tummy

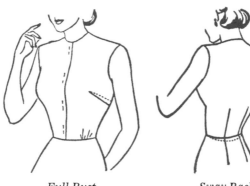

Full Bust   Sway Back

Project Checklist

Project name: _____

Date started: _____

Project description: _____

_____

Occasion/use: _____

Measurements: _____

_____

_____

_____

_____

Fabrics: _____

_____

_____

Thread type: _____

Interfacing type: _____

Needle type: _____

Special notions needed: _____

_____

_____

Apron With "Built-In" Towel

A relatively simple idea has corrected an age-old problem for me and proved to be a profitable idea as well. Like most housewives, I had the habit of drying my hands on the side of my apron when I was very busy. This made quite a mess of the apron. Now I buy a 25 cent hand towel (the type with fringe on each end). When I make an apron, I cut off the fringe from one end of the towel near the ribbing, and this piece I cut in lengths to trim the apron pocket. The end of the towel, which is now plain, I pleat into four pleats with pins and sew to the waistband on the left side of the apron. I stitch it on so that when the band is turned and stitched the final time, it covers the top of the towel. By cutting some material off the top of the towel, you can shorten it for a child's apron. Each apron costs me less than 70 cents to make, and they sell for $1.50 to $1.75. Our church group also made a nice sum of money by selling them.

— Mrs. Kenneth Stamper

From "Women Who Make Cents"
February 1957 issue of *The WORKBASKET*

My Design

Title: _____

Date started: _____

Project description: _____

_____

Occasion/use: _____

Measurements: _____

_____

Fabrics: _____

_____

_____

Notions: _____

Special notes: _____

_____

Changes to original concept: _____

_____

_____

Date completed: _____

fabric

DATE: _____

SOURCE: _____

YARDAGE: _____

COST: _____

DATE: _____

SOURCE: _____

YARDAGE: _____

COST: _____

DATE: _____

SOURCE: _____

YARDAGE: _____

COST: _____

DATE: _____

SOURCE: _____

YARDAGE: _____

COST: _____

DATE: _____

SOURCE: _____

YARDAGE: _____

COST: _____

DATE: _____

SOURCE: _____

YARDAGE: _____

COST: _____

DATE: _____

SOURCE: _____

YARDAGE: _____

COST: _____

DATE: _____

SOURCE: _____

YARDAGE: _____

COST: _____

Gifts IN A *Jiff*

DATE MADE/NEEDED: . . . .

OCCASION:. . . . .

FOR WHOM:. . . . .

PROJECT DESCRIPTION:. . . . .

. . . .

MATERIALS: . . . .

. . . .

COST PER GIFT: . . . .

Triumphs

	COMPLETED DATE
1. _____	
2. _____	
3. _____	
4. _____	
5. _____	

· ·

Conquer

	GOAL DATE
1. _____	
2. _____	
3. _____	
4. _____	
5. _____	

BASIC SEWING SKILLS

✳ Running Stitch—To make this stitch, push the point of the needle in and out of the fabric until you have several stitches on the needle. Hold the fabric taut with your left hand, and pull the needle through. Practice until you make fine even stitches.

✳ Backstitch—Make one running stitch, then take a stitch back to the beginning of the first stitch, thus overlapping each running stitch. Resembles machine stitching and is used to strengthen a seam made by hand.

✳ Overcasting—This is for sewing over and over of edges to prevent raveling and fraying. Work from right to left and make stitches about ⅛" deep and ¼" apart.

✳ Basting—Basting is quite important in successful sewing. This is used to hold fabric temporarily in place, until it can be permanently stitched. There are four types of basting: hand basting, machine basting, pin basting and basting edges with an iron.

  ✳ Hand Basting is made by making longer running stitches. A glazed or waxed thread that will not snarl is best, because usually a long length is used.

  ✳ Machine Basting is quite popular now, because the stitch on most new sewing machines is so easy to regulate. Simply lengthen the stitch and loosen the tension. It holds ruffles and gathers in place and helps to keep bias edges from stretching.

  ✳ Pin Basting is used more on long, straight seams. Place the pins at right angles to the seam edge with the pin heads to the right, thus making it easy to remove the pins when stitching. Be careful not to pull or stretch the fabric as you work. However, most new machines sew over pins, or a hinged foot can be placed on an old machine to make this possible.

  ✳ Pressing Seams with an iron is used mostly to hold straight edges such as pocket seams, yokes or hems. Simply turn under the desired amount of fabric and press.

✳ Hemming—The open side of the hem is held toward you. Work from right to left, and catch a very small stitch in the garment and a slightly deeper stitch in the hem. You want to achieve as nearly as possible an invisible stitch on the right side. These stitches may be made close together for greater strength or spaced farther apart.

✳ Slipstitch—A kind of hemming stitch. The stitches on both right and wrong sides should be practically invisible. Take a small stitch in the garment, run the point of needle in the fold of hem about ¼", pull out fabric and continue as before. Hems are sometimes slipstitched, and linings are fastened to inside of coats in this manner.

✳ Catchstitch—This is used for a flat finish next to fabric, such as seam binding on a hem. Hold the open hem edge away from you, and work from left to right. Take a stitch in the hem, then a tiny stitch to the right, just beyond the edge of the hem with the point of needle to the left. This makes diagonal lines that cross each other.

May 1951

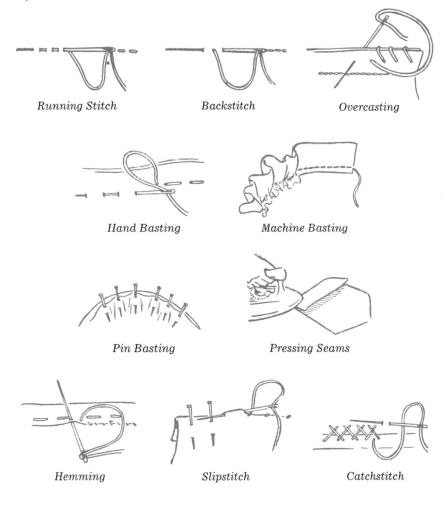

Running Stitch   Backstitch   Overcasting

Hand Basting   Machine Basting

Pin Basting   Pressing Seams

Hemming   Slipstitch   Catchstitch

BASIC SEAMS

✳ Plain Seam—Stitch two pieces of fabric together, open the seam and press flat.

✳ Topstitched Seam—A row of stitching is added on top of each side of a plain seam.

✳ French Seam—Stitch along half of the seam allowance on the right side of the garment, then trim the seam close to the stitching line ¼" to ⅜". Turn to the wrong side and make a second row of stitching on the seam line. Used on infants' wear, lingerie, some blouses and pillow slips.

✳ Flat Fell—Place the right sides of the fabric together and stitch the seam the desired width. Trim one edge to within ⅛" of the stitching. Turn the other edge in and stitch flat over trimmed blouses, slacks or anyplace a strong seam is desired.

✳ Double-Stitched Seam—A plain seam that has been stitched twice—once on the seam line and again ⅛" from the first stitching. Used on armhole seams, bias seams and other places where strength is needed.

✳ Overcast Seam—Make stitches about ⅛" deep and about ¼" apart over the edges of the seams to prevent fraying.

✳ Pinking—To pink seams, use pinking shears, a pinking attachment or hand pink with scissors by cutting sharp notches along the edge.

✳ Bound Seam—Each edge of the seam is bound with bias binding and the seam pressed open. Makes a neat inside seam finish for unlined coats and other tailored garments.

✳ Hemmed Seam—Press a plain seam open, turn the edge under about ⅛" and stitch close to the edge. Used on lightweight fabrics. Another seam finish is made by turning the edges of the seam in toward each other and then sewing them together with running stitches.

June 1951

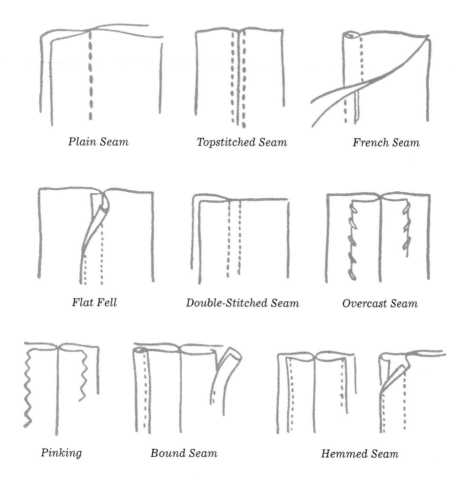

Plain Seam

Topstitched Seam

French Seam

Flat Fell

Double-Stitched Seam

Overcast Seam

Pinking

Bound Seam

Hemmed Seam

Project Checklist

Project name: _____

Date started: _____

Project description: _____

_____

Occasion/use: _____

Measurements: _____

_____

_____

_____

_____

Fabrics: _____

_____

_____

Thread type: _____

Interfacing type: _____

Needle type: _____

Special notions needed: _____

_____

_____

Hand-Decorated Buttons

I decorate ordinary plain buttons with simple floral, block print or children's designs. Plain, self-shank variety in pearl, plastic or wood is preferable. Run a wire hairpin through the shank and twist the ends together to form a handle to use while decorating. Buttons with a shiny surface are given a coat of clear nail polish and allowed to dry before decorating. Use a set of wood-covered watercolor pencils, keeping the point slightly wet, when applying color. The more moisture used, the more brilliant the color will be. When dry, apply one or more coats of clear nail polish and allow to dry. This protects the color so the button will stand careful laundering, but it's a good idea to twist a bit of kitchen foil over each button before laundering or cleaning. Six buttons to a card sell for $1 to $3 per set, depending on the cost of the buttons and the amount of handwork required.

— Helen LeMunyon

From "Women Who Make Cents"
June 1964 issue of The WORKBASKET

My Design

Title: _____

Date started: _____

Project description: _____

_____

Occasion/use: _____

Measurements: _____

_____

Fabrics: _____

_____

_____

Notions: _____

Special notes: _____

_____

Changes to original concept: _____

_____

_____

Date completed: _____

fabric

DATE: _____

SOURCE: _____

YARDAGE: _____

COST: _____

DATE: _____

SOURCE: _____

YARDAGE: _____

COST: _____

DATE: _____

SOURCE: _____

YARDAGE: _____

COST: _____

DATE: _____

SOURCE: _____

YARDAGE: _____

COST: _____

DATE: _____

SOURCE: _____

YARDAGE: _____

COST: _____

DATE: _____

SOURCE: _____

YARDAGE: _____

COST: _____

DATE: _____

SOURCE: _____

YARDAGE: _____

COST: _____

DATE: _____

SOURCE: _____

YARDAGE: _____

COST: _____

Gifts IN A Jiff

DATE MADE/NEEDED: . . . .

OCCASION:. . . . .

FOR WHOM:. . . . .

PROJECT DESCRIPTION:. . . . .

. . . .

MATERIALS: . . . .

. . . .

COST PER GIFT: . . . .

Needle Pointers

✳ A good rule for ruffles is to make them three times the desired finished length for very full and sheer ruffles and one-and-a-half times the finished length for dresses and aprons made of cotton print goods. Bias ruffle can be made less full.

December 1953

✳ When putting two pockets on a garment fold the garment in the center, placing one pocket in the right position and pin on the garment, pinning both sides together. Stitch around the pocket with the machine unthreaded. Then unpin and you have a pattern on each side for placing pockets.

November 1940

✳ Buttons that must do heavy duty will stay on longer if they have some "play" in them. Here's one method for sewing them on: place a thick darning needle across the top of the button so the thread goes over it, and stitch the button down as usual. When finished, take out the darning needle, pull the button up so the threads are snug at the top and wind thread firmly around the "stem" between the button and the garment.

April 1956

✳ When a machine-stitched seam breaks in a garment, the proper hand method for repairing it is the backstitch. Work stitches very small and close together, taking care to follow the original seam line and to stretch the material so it won't pucker.

May 1956

✳ When hemming a full skirt, cut a width of cardboard the desired width of the hem. Go around the skirt with this, turning up the hem the width of the cardboard and pinning every 3" or less. Then baste and proceed as usual. This method will speed the job considerably.

August 1956

✳ On facings (collars, for example), "blend" the seam by trimming one side of the seam narrower than the other. Pressing then will not leave a definite line revealing the seam edges.

November 1956

Triumphs

	COMPLETED DATE
1.	
2.	
3.	
4.	
5.	

. . . .

Conquer

	GOAL DATE
1.	
2.	
3.	
4.	
5.	

VARIOUS KINDS OF HEMS

Hems are quite important in finishing any garment. They can be decorative or inconspicuous. Hand hems show less than machine hems and are used on fine garments. To make a plain hem, turn the material to the wrong side and fold over the raw edge about ¼"; turn a second fold the desired width of the hem.

❋ A Hem Gauge is essential to ensure an even hem.

❋ Felling-stitch Hem is the most common stitch used for hemming. It is made by sewing the hem from right to left and working toward you. Take a tiny stitch in the garment and a tiny stitch in the folded edge of the hem—catch only one or two threads on the garment side; these stitches are rather slanting.

❋ Blind Hems are used when an invisible hem on the right side is desired. Use the felling stitch, working with matching thread. Space the stitches about ⅜" apart and do not take up more than one thread of the garment with each stitch.

❋ Slipstitched Hem is used for facings and for hemming the linings in coats and dresses. Using thread that matches the fabric, take a stitch in the garment, pick up one thread (in woolen fabric, this stitch should catch only the top threads and not go through), then insert the needle through the underside of the folded edge, and slip it along inside the fold until you are ready to make the next stitch. Do not draw the thread tight and make the stitches about ¼" apart.

❋ Hand-rolled Hems are most suitable for use on sheer fabric and can be made on the bias or straight of the material. Use a fine needle and thread. Roll the edge of the fabric between your thumb and first finger (moistening the fingers will help). Hem with fine, even felling stitches.

❋ Shell Hem is a decorative hem used mostly on underwear. Baste a narrow hem about ¼" or less, depending on the fabric and how it will be used. With matching thread take two or three overcast stitches over the hem, pull tight, hem the edge for about ½", then repeat the overcasting stitches.

❋ Circular Hems are used in hemming flared skirts. First baste the finished edge line of the skirt, turn the edge ½" and gather it, then turn the hem and lay it flat, hemming it to the garment. Or gather the edge without turning it, using a running stitch, and finish with bias tape;

then fold and fasten to the garment on the wrong side. If hemming a curved edge, make a narrow hem ½" or less. However if the skirt edge is quite full, circular-stitched hems 1" wide are very pretty.

✳ In hemming a skirt with box pleats, clip the seam edges at the point where the hem will come, open the seams and press flat. Turn the hem edge using a running or machine stitch, then hem by hand. Excess fullness can be laid in small darts on both sides of the pleat.

✳ Taped Hems can be used on practically all fabrics; however they are especially desirable for woolens. Do not make the first turn; instead place the seam binding on the right side of the raw edge, stitch completely around the hem, then hem to the garment on the wrong side with invisible stitches.

July and August 1951

Hand-rolled Hem

Hem Gauge

Shell Hem

Felling-stitch Hem

Circular Hem

Blind Hem

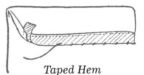

Pleated Skirt Hem

Slipstitched Hem

Taped Hem

Project Checklist

Project name: _____

Date started: _____

Project description: _____

_____

Occasion/use: _____

Measurements: _____

_____

_____

_____

_____

Fabrics: _____

_____

_____

Thread type: _____

Interfacing type: _____

Needle type: _____

Special notions needed: _____

_____

_____

Beaded Blouses

Five years ago I was stricken with an incurable spinal disease that is a very progressive crippler. Of course, I had to quit work, and I immediately began to think what I might do. All my life I have liked to sew, and I decided that I would see if I could supplement my income in this way. I bought some tissue faille, a basic blouse pattern, a beading transfer pattern and some beads. When I finished my first blouse, I used it as a sample, and the results were amazing. In a small way, I had gone into business for myself. My blouses range in price from $8 to $15, depending on the design used. I furnish all the materials needed for the blouse, and my customer has a wide variety of colors and beading designs to choose from. This has proved to be a successful venture.

— Mrs. Sara E. Quinn

From "Women Who Make Cents"
October 1953 issue of The WORKBASKET

75

My Design

Title: _____

Date started: _____

Project description: _____

_____

Occasion/use: _____

Measurements: _____

_____

Fabrics: _____

_____

_____

Notions: _____

Special notes: _____

_____

Changes to original concept: _____

_____

_____

Date completed: _____

fabric

DATE: _____

SOURCE: _____

YARDAGE: _____

COST: _____

DATE: _____

SOURCE: _____

YARDAGE: _____

COST: _____

DATE: _____

SOURCE: _____

YARDAGE: _____

COST: _____

DATE: _____

SOURCE: _____

YARDAGE: _____

COST: _____

DATE: _____

SOURCE: _____

YARDAGE: _____

COST: _____

DATE: _____

SOURCE: _____

YARDAGE: _____

COST: _____

DATE: _____

SOURCE: _____

YARDAGE: _____

COST: _____

DATE: _____

SOURCE: _____

YARDAGE: _____

COST: _____

Gifts IN A Jiff

DATE MADE/NEEDED: . . . .

OCCASION:. . . . .

FOR WHOM: . . . .

PROJECT DESCRIPTION: . . . .

. . . .

MATERIALS: . . . .

. . . .

COST PER GIFT: . . . .

Triumphs

	COMPLETED DATE
1.	
2.	
3.	
4.	
5.	

· ·

Conquer

	GOAL DATE
1.	
2.	
3.	
4.	
5.	

Project Checklist

Project name: _____

Date started: _____

Project description: _____

_____

Occasion/use: _____

Measurements: _____

_____

_____

_____

_____

Fabrics: _____

_____

_____

Thread type: _____

Interfacing type: _____

Needle type: _____

Special notions needed: _____

_____

_____

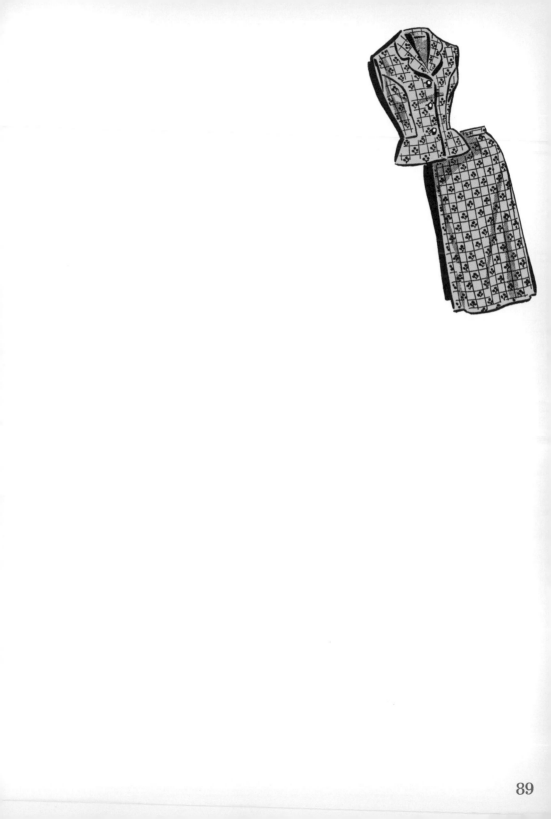

FACINGS

Curtains, drapes and other home decorations, as well as garments, need facings. They are used at the neckline, skirt hem, sleeve edge, front of the jacket or coat or blouse, or wherever there is not enough material to turn a hem. The seams may be stitched by hand or by machine; turn the machine facings so they will not show. Some facings are cut with the garments and are turned back; others are cut the same as the garment edges, stitched and folded back. If the edge is straight, the facing should be cut on the straight of goods; if edge curves, the facing should be on the true bias or an exact duplication of the curve of the edge.

✳ Straight Facings are used to turn an edge smoothly when it is not possible to spare fabric for a hem. They can be turned as facings on the wrong side or used as trimming bands on right side. When the facing is to be turned on the wrong side, apply a straight strip of fabric on the right side of the garment. Stitch the facing and the edge of garment in a seam. Turn to the wrong side and baste the seamed edge. Turn the edge of the facing under and hem to garment.

✳ Shaped Facings are cut to duplicate the edge of the garment or are cut in one with the garment and folded back to resemble a facing.

✳ Scalloped Facing—To face a scalloped edge, baste the straight edge of the facing to the edge of the material to be scalloped. Then mark the scallops' desired size, using a scallop marker, glass, cup or spool. Stitch along the outline into each point of the curve. Trim the seam and clip curved seams. Turn to the right side exactly on the seam edge, baste and press each scallop. Turn the edge of the facing under and hem to the fabric.

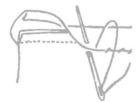

Straight Facing

Shaped Facing

Scalloped Facing

✴ Square Neck Facing—With right sides together, baste or pin the bias or straight facing to the garment. Cut the corners of the facing to match the neckline or garment and stitch. Trim and slash the corners, turn to the wrong side. Press and stitch around the edge of the facing if desired. If the outer edges are not stitched, turn the raw edges under and slipstitch.

✴ Round Neck Facing—Baste or pin the facing to the garment. Stitch, clip the curved parts of the seam, trim and turn to the wrong side. Press and baste the folded edge at the neckline, turn the edge of the facing tack, and blindstitch or machine-stitch to the garment.

✴ V-neck Facing—With right sides together, baste the facing to the garment; allow plenty of material to mitre at the point. Stitch the ends of the facing and press open the seam at the point. Stitch about ¼" from the edge around the neckline. Slash the corners, turn the facing to the wrong side. Machine-stitch or tack to the garment.

Square Neck Facing

Round Neck Facing

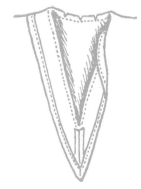

V-neck Facing

Facings continued on page 92»

✳ Curved Collar with Bias Binding—Pin and baste the under edge of the collar to the neckline, slightly snug to prevent buckling. Baste the bias edging along the upper edge of the collar and stitch. Turn, baste and blindstitch to the wrong side.

✳ Round Collar with Bias Strip—Cut a bias strip about 1½" wide, baste to the collar and neckline, and stitch. Turn the collar and binding. Make about a ½" turn on the binding and baste, then blindstitch to the garment.

✳ Standing Collar with Faced Front Opening—Stitch the collar at each end and clip, trim the corners, turn and press. With right sides together, stitch the facing to the front of the garment. Pin the seams of the collar and front opening, baste and stitch the inner edge of the collar to the neckline of the garment. Clip the seam, press and turn the collar and facing the right side out. Baste-turned edges, press and blindstitch the collar to the stitching of the neckline at the back. Turn the inner edge of the facing, and stitch to the garment.

September 1951

*Curved Collar
with Bias Binding*

*Round Collar
with Bias Strip*

*Standing Collar with
Faced Front Opening*

Clutch Bag

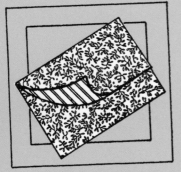

A cute clutch bag can be easily made from left-over material. Take an 8" ×20" piece of material, fold it in half, sew up the sides and hem the top. To make it reversible, follow the same steps, then put one bag inside the other and sew the tops together. This is a good way to use leftover dress material to make a matching purse. By reversing it, the other side can match still another outfit. More or less material can be used for the desired size, and pockets can be added outside. These can be easily sold to friends for $1 (letting them select their own material) or given away as gifts.

— *Mrs. Helen E. Painter*

From "Women Who Make Cents"
November 1963 issue of *The WORKBASKET*

97

My Design

Title: _____

Date started: _____

Project description: _____

_____

Occasion/use: _____

Measurements: _____

_____

Fabrics: _____

_____

_____

Notions: _____

Special notes: _____

_____

Changes to original concept: _____

_____

_____

Date completed: _____

fabric

DATE: _____

SOURCE: _____

YARDAGE: _____

COST: _____

DATE: _____

SOURCE: _____

YARDAGE: _____

COST: _____

DATE: _____

SOURCE: _____

YARDAGE: _____

COST: _____

DATE: _____

SOURCE: _____

YARDAGE: _____

COST: _____

DATE: _____

SOURCE: _____

YARDAGE: _____

COST: _____

DATE: _____

SOURCE: _____

YARDAGE: _____

COST: _____

DATE: _____

SOURCE: _____

YARDAGE: _____

COST: _____

DATE: _____

SOURCE: _____

YARDAGE: _____

COST: _____

Gifts IN A Jiff

DATE MADE/NEEDED: . . . .

OCCASION:. . . . .

FOR WHOM:. . . . .

PROJECT DESCRIPTION:. . . . .

. . . .

MATERIALS: . . . .

. . . .

COST PER GIFT: . . . .

VARIOUS KINDS OF EDGE FINISHES

✳ Bias fold, available at all notion counters in a variety of colors, is probably one of the most popular bindings used. It can be sewed to the edge of a piece of cloth using the binder attachment. Only one row of stitching is needed because the edge of the cloth and both edges of the fold are caught in the row of stitching. (Figure 1)

✳ If you are cutting your own bias binding, allow twice the width of the finished binding plus the seam allowance. Stretch the bias strips slightly while pinning to the material. Place the right side of the binding next to the right side of the garment, stitch along the edge of the right side, turn the binding over the seam to the wrong side, turn the raw edges under and hem with invisible stitches. (Figure 2)

✳ A French-rolled edge is simply a bias strip folded in half. The two cut edges of the fold are stitched on the right side of the edge to be finished. Then turn the fold over the seam and hem on the wrong side with invisible stitches, or catch in the machine stitches. This type of edge is often used around the necks of blouses, sleeve edges or on children's dresses. (Figure 3)

✳ Decorative trims such as rickrack are quite popular. Turn and press the seam allowance to the wrong side. Lay the edge on the center of the rickrack and stitch. For narrow rickrack, one row of stitching is sufficient; two rows are necessary for wider rickrack, so as to catch points on the wrong side to make ironing easier. (Figure 4)

✳ A ruffled lace edge is made by pulling one of the straight threads along the top of the lace to form tiny gathers. Or whip over the fine edge with fine thread and long stitches, then draw up the whipping thread. Hold the lace toward you and against the right side of the fabric. With small whipping or overcast stitches, sew to the edge of collars, cuffs, yokes or wherever desired. As you sew, ease the fullness with the thumb of your left hand. When you are finished, turn the lace edge down and press it neatly. (Figure 5)

✳ Corded or piped edges are very decorative and are used on sport jackets, slipcovers, pajamas, pillows, tailored garments and many other uses. Various sizes of cable cord can be purchased. To cover, cut a bias strip wide enough to cover the cord and allow ½" for the seam. Fold the bias piece right-side out and in half over the cord. You may wish to baste for stitching, but it is not necessary. Guard against stretching the bias strips when sewing. Place the covered cord on the edge to be trimmed so it is just inside the seam allowance. Pin in place. Baste through the seam line, catching both the seam allowance of the cord and fabric underneath. Stitch with a cording foot along the basting. Be careful going around corners and curves to avoid puckering. (Figure 6)

✳ Bands of varying width and colors are often used to finish edges. Bias bands of plaids or contrasting colors are used for decoration on cuffs and neck openings. The right side of the band is stitched to the wrong side of the garment, then turned to the right side. Press the seam edge and stitch along the top of the band. Bands are also placed flat on previous parts of the garment. Simply turn the edges under and stitch. (Figure 7)

✳ A picot edge is used most frequently on pillow slips and around the lower edge of blouses and slips. Mark the desired line for hemstitching; hemstitch and cut through the center of the hemstitching. (Figure 8)

October 1951

Figure 1

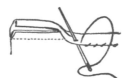

Figure 2

Figure 3

Figure 4

Figure 5

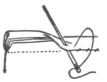

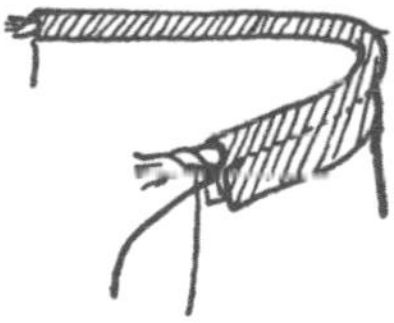

Figure 6

Figure 7

Figure 8

Triumphs

	COMPLETED DATE
1. _____	
2. _____	
3. _____	
4. _____	
5. _____	

· ·

Conquer

	GOAL DATE
1. _____	
2. _____	
3. _____	
4. _____	
5. _____	

Little Coats from Big Ones

While recovering from a nervous breakdown, I thought of a new way to earn some money without having to work away from home. I decided to cash in on an old pastime of mine—sewing. It occurred to me that many women with children would welcome the opportunity to have children's coats made from their discarded large ones, so I inserted an advertisement in our small neighborhood newspaper, which read as follows: "Child's beautifully tailored coat made from your discarded large one, only $3.50." The response was terrific, and I soon found my house overflowing with coats of all descriptions. The price seems ridiculously small, but I am able to make a good profit by cutting and sewing several at a time. To anyone who can sew, this work is not at all difficult and excellent results can be obtained. The large coat must first be cleaned, then it is taken completely apart and cut over a child's pattern, cutting around the worn spots. Sometimes when a coat is worn, it is possible to turn the material, using the inside for the outside of the child's coat. I have achieved such fine results that people often cannot believe they were made from old coats. And I have the satisfaction of knowing that my hobby is a worthwhile one.

— *Miss Mildred S. Wiltser*

From "Women Who Make Cents"
January 1953 issue of *The* WORKBASKET

SHOULDER AND SLEEVE TECHNIQUES

One of the most common alterations to make is in the length and the position of the shoulder line. This must be done on the pattern; do not add or take off at the bottom or top of the sleeve or at the armscye.

It is important to check your own sleeve length and the length of the pattern. Lay the pattern flat and measure from the top perforation of the sleeve straight down to the lower edge, as shown in Figure 1a. To get a sleeve length, measure from the top of the shoulder, with the elbow bent, down around the elbow to the wrist, as shown in Figure 1b. Now compare these measurements. If the sleeve is too long, fold the pattern below and above the elbow, as shown in Figure 2. Be careful and do not take up too much because some sleeves should blouse at the wrist. To add length, cut and spread the pattern, like in Figure 3.

Figure 1a   Figure 1b

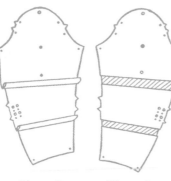

Figure 2   Figure 3   Figure 4   Figure 5

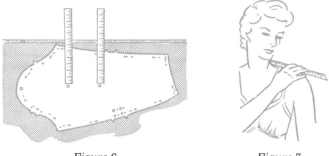

Figure 6　　　　　　　　　　*Figure 7*

No sleeve fits comfortably or hangs correctly if it is not cut right. Read and reread the instruction sheet; be sure you know what each marking and perforation means. If it is possible, cut both sleeves at the same time. If you must cut them one at a time, make sure that both sleeves are not cut for the same armhole.

For a heavy upper arm, cut and spread the pattern, as shown in Figure 4. Increase the desired width at the top, tapering to the wrist; be sure to add to the blouse pattern at the underarm.

Figure 5 shows laying a pleat in a pattern if the sleeve is too large for a thin arm.

The perforations marking the length of the pattern should be placed with the lengthwise thread of the material. This can be easily checked by measuring from each perforation to the selvage or straight outer edge, as shown in Figure 6. Pin the pattern to the material. Use even strokes when cutting; cut all notches out.

The length and position of the shoulder line is also important. This seam actually holds the garment in place. For this measurement, measure from the highest point at the neckline to ½" back of the highest point on the tip of the shoulder. Take a pencil or ruler and lay it from the correct point at the neckline to the correct one at the tip of the shoulder, as shown in Figure 7. This line should not be visible from the front or back, and the garment should not hang to the front or back. For rounded shoulders, place the seams farther back of the normal shoulder. To do this, take off the back and add to the front by basting tissue to the pattern where needed. Shoulders of some individuals may slope or be straighter than the average.

September 1952

SLEEVES AND ARMHOLES

✳ One-Piece Sleeve—Fullness at the elbow may be taken care of in three ways: unstitched pleats, darts or gathers (Figure 1).

✳ Two-Piece Sleeve—This type of sleeve is most frequently used in coats and suits. The slight fullness at the elbow (Figure 2) should be shrunk out by steam pressing after finely gathering between the notches.

✳ Raglan Sleeve—Join the diagonal seams to the blouse before the underarm seam on the blouse and sleeves are joined (Figure 3). Clip the seams every inch at the curved position.

✳ Epaulet Sleeve—This type of sleeve is nice for woolen fabric (Figure 4). Stitch the underarm seam of the sleeve. Join the sleeve to the armhole, holding it toward you; pin, baste and stitch to where the epaulet begins. Clip at the corners, turn the edges under the epaulet (turn the sleeve to the right side) and pin. Be sure you match notches.

✳ Kimono Sleeve—A portion of the shoulder line and underarm seam are extended on the bodice to form a slight cap (Figure 5). The underarm seam is curved and needs to be snipped so it will not pucker on the right side. Some kimono sleeves, especially if closely fitted, need a gusset under the arm to allow for freedom and to protect the sleeve from tearing out. To insert the gusset, cut a slash about 3" deep at right angles to the seam at the top of the underarm (Figure 6a). Cut away a

Figure 1:
One-Piece Sleeve

Figure 2:
Two-Piece Sleeve

Figure 3:
Raglan Sleeve

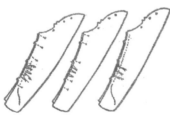

Figure 4: Epaulet Sleeve

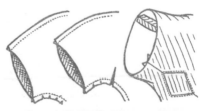

Figures 5, 6a, 6b: Kimono Sleeve

portion of the material if desired. You may stitch around the opening if desired. Cut a diamond-shaped bias piece large enough to cover the slash. Turn the edge of the opening under. Place the gusset on the wrong side under the opening, pin, baste and stitch. A completed gusset is shown in Figure 6b.

✳ Square Armhole—The sleeve is darted at the top (Figure 7). With the sleeve toward you, pin in the armhole, matching notches, underarm seams and shoulders. Ease in the fullness, baste and stitch. Slit the corners and treat carefully so they will be perfect.

✳ Pointed Armhole—The top of the sleeve that fits into a pointed armhole has a dart-like seam; press the seam open before it is joined to the armhole. The sleeve is set in the same manner as the others (Figure 8).

✳ Darts at Top of Sleeve—Some dress patterns have darts at the top; however they are used more on suits and coats. These are stitched to points, then pressed toward the center. Hold the sleeve toward you and pin it to the armhole, matching seams and notches (Figure 9).

✳ Gathered Top Sleeve—Make about three rows of stitching, then pull to the size of the armhole. Distribute the gathers evenly. Insert in the armhole and hold the sleeve toward you and pin, matching notches, shoulder and underarms. Pin, baste and stitch along the top, gathering the thread (Figure 10).

October 1952

Figure 7: Square Armhole

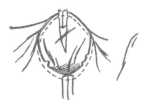

Figure 8: Pointed Armhole

Figure 9: Darts at Top of Sleeve

Figure 10: Gathered Top Sleeve

Project Checklist

Project name: _____

Date started: _____

Project description: _____

_____

Occasion/use: _____

Measurements: _____

_____

_____

_____

_____

Fabrics: _____

_____

_____

Thread type: _____

Interfacing type: _____

Needle type: _____

Special notions needed: _____

_____

_____

My Design

Title: _____

Date started: _____

Project description: _____

_____

Occasion/use: _____

Measurements: _____

_____

Fabrics: _____

_____

_____

Notions: _____

Special notes: _____

_____

Changes to original concept: _____

_____

_____

Date completed: _____

Glitterbags

Glitterbags sell well all year long, but are especially popular during the heavy summer driving months. I make mine of felt decorated with the words "Keep America Clean" spelled out in sequins. The bags must be large enough to hold a brown paper bag, which lines them and is, of course, disposable. I make them with loop handles so they may be hung beneath the dash. The bags are simple and fairly quick to make. Done in colors to harmonize with the auto interiors, these sell for $1.25 each.

— *Mrs. Leonard Langhorst*

From "Women Who Make Cents"
August 1960 issue of *The WORKBASKET*

fabric

DATE: _____

SOURCE: _____

YARDAGE: _____

COST: _____

DATE: _____

SOURCE: _____

YARDAGE: _____

COST: _____

DATE: _____

SOURCE: _____

YARDAGE: _____

COST: _____

DATE: _____

SOURCE: _____

YARDAGE: _____

COST: _____

DATE: _____

SOURCE: _____

YARDAGE: _____

COST: _____

DATE: _____

SOURCE: _____

YARDAGE: _____

COST: _____

DATE: _____

SOURCE: _____

YARDAGE: _____

COST: _____

DATE: _____

SOURCE: _____

YARDAGE: _____

COST: _____

Gifts IN A *Jiff*

DATE MADE/NEEDED: . . . .

OCCASION: . . . .

FOR WHOM: . . . .

PROJECT DESCRIPTION: . . . .

. . . .

MATERIALS: . . . .

. . . .

COST PER GIFT: . . . .

Triumphs

	COMPLETED DATE
1. _____	
2. _____	
3. _____	
4. _____	
5. _____	

. . . .

Conquer

	GOAL DATE
1. _____	
2. _____	
3. _____	
4. _____	
5. _____	

Needle Pointers

* Fasten loose ends of thread to the spool with a bit of cellophane tape—saves wasted minutes untangling the thread box.

August 1954

* Here's a time- and motion-saver when you're starting a sewing project: fill all the bobbins you will need before you begin; then there will be no stopping to rethread the machine.

August 1954

* Used and discarded shoulder pads make satisfactory extra pin cushions for such places in the house as closets, the laundry room and kitchen. Cover with a scrap of material and dress them up with bias seam binding around the seams. Larger sizes may be fastened around the wrist with a loop and button, or hook and eye, for use in dress-making projects.

February 1955

* When you machine-stitch jersey material (rayon or any other material), keep the tension loose and stretch the fabric a little as you stitch so the seam itself will have some stretch to it. Always use fine needles for either hand- or machine-stitching of jersey.

August 1955

* If you have several of the same garment to be cut out of material—such as choir robes, costumes and the like—you will save much time by putting several thicknesses of material (up to four) together and cutting all at the same time. Pin the layers together, lay out the pattern on top and cut as you would a single thickness.

May 1956

* Here's a handy method for keeping embroidery thread in good condition. Place the thread in envelopes in a card file and classify according to color and number.

May 1958

* In sewing, it is best to cut cotton thread rather than break it because breaking weakens the thread.

June 1962

BOUND BUTTONHOLES

Do you enjoy making bound buttonholes? Do you glory in their sharply pressed, square beauty? Oh! You've never dared to tackle a bound buttonhole? Pick up your courage, and let's go out for a practice run! It's sheer fun, and the result is a delight to the home dressmaker's eye. Besides, bound buttonholes are strong and can be made over worked buttonholes to rejuvenate them.

You have marked with basting thread or chalk the line where the buttonhole is to go; usually you will make more than one, so mark all at once. Cut a strip of fabric about an 1½" wider than the length the finished buttonhole is to be, thus allowing ¾" at each end of this strip, which becomes the binding. This should be on the straight of the fabric or the true bias for a trim. Mark it for buttonholes to correspond with the garment (Figure 1)—patterns usually are perforated for this. If you prefer, you may cut out separate pieces to bind each buttonhole, but it is easier with a strip, which is later snipped and trimmed. Place the right side of the binding over the right side of the buttonhole, lining up the basting marks on each. With your machine, begin in the center of the buttonhole and run a line of fine stitches around the marking of the buttonhole (usually the width of presser foot from the center on each side and straight across each end), turning nice, square corners at the end (Figure 2). This is accomplished by leaving the machine needle down in the fabric; then lift the presser foot, turn the garment and continue with the other side or end—this makes a perfectly square corner. Count the number of stitches across each end. For a small buttonhole, run the stitching as close together as possible, so when the cut is made, the stitches will hold the fabric from raveling.

To make the cut, you may prefer to use buttonhole scissors; start at the center, between the stitching, and cut to within ¼" or ⅜" of each end (Figure 3). At the ends, make diagonal cuts to the corners, cutting right up to the stitching line, but not through the thread (Figure 4). If you have used a binding strip, cut it about ¾" from each edge (Figure 4), and turn the binding through the buttonhole to the wrong side or back of the garment (Figure 5). Draw all into shape, observing from the right side that the binding is turned back evenly and exactly the right distance to make a fine, straight finish (Figure 6). Make sure that the ends of the buttonholes are pulled out even. Make an inverted pleat at each end on the under side. Fasten triangular pieces at the ends of the binding with a few stitches (Figure 7). Flatten with fingers, pin and baste, then press.

Cut the facing through the buttonhole, turn the edges under the slipstitch or hem down to the buttonhole, keeping the corners square and the edges of the binding close together with easy diagonal stitches (Figure 8), and finish pressing.

The same procedure goes for buttonholes that you desire to renovate, except that more care must be used to keep the work flat and true. Keeping the binding uncut until stitching is completed will help. A finishing stitch may be used on the right side, if desired; it should be made with very fine stitches.

Corded Buttonholes—Cut two corded pieces, stitching or basting to hold the cord, 1" longer than the buttonhole. Trim the raw edge to about ⅛" before stitching. Stitch both strips to the right side of the material, having the raw edges meet in the center (Figure 9). Do not stitch across the ends. Cut between stitchings and diagonally to the corner. Turn the corded strip through the slash to the wrong side. Stitch across the triangular ends to the ends of the cording (Figure 10). Face and finish the same as for bound buttonholes.

March 1952

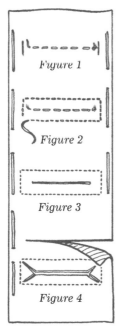

Figure 1

Figure 2

Figure 3

Figure 4

Figure 5

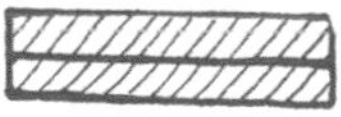

Figure 6

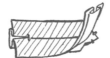

Figure 7

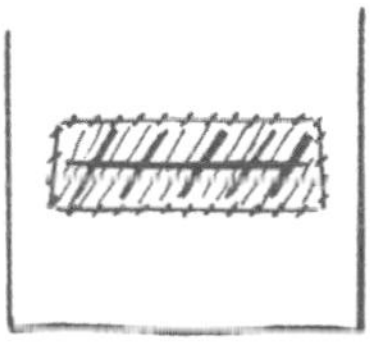

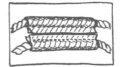

Figure 8

Figure 9

Figure 10

Project Checklist

Project name: _____

Date started: _____

Project description: _____
_____

Occasion/use: _____

Measurements: _____
_____
_____
_____
_____

Fabrics: _____
_____
_____

Thread type: _____

Interfacing type: _____

Needle type: _____

Special notions needed: _____
_____
_____

Business in Boleros

The handiest article of clothing in my wardrobe during the spring and summer seasons is a brief bolero, made to match or contrast with sundresses and sports outfits, with a large initial or monogram embroidered on it to make it personally mine. Some of my friends asked me to make up these boleros for them, and it has become quite a thriving business for me about this time of year. Most popular fabrics are white pique or white, green, navy or red linen or butcher linen. Some women bring their own materials to match a dress they are making. A favorite combination is a white pique bolero with red and blue monogram. The patterns I use are some I purchased in the pattern department of a local department store. I chose two styles, one a sleeveless loose bolero and one with set-in sleeves, five buttons down the front, and a short point in the center back. I charge from $2 to $5 for the labor, depending on the style and amount embroidery involved. I use the simplest of outline and herringbone embroidery stitches, but they are the most effective. Also, for a young girl, I have made two or three boleros with tiny collars out of taffeta and embroidered with sequins or beads (pearls on soft blue are really effective) to go over her formal gowns.

— *Beverly A. Angel*

From "Women Who Make Cents"
May 1951 issue of *The WORKBASKET*

My Design

Title: _____

Date started: _____

Project description: _____

_____

Occasion/use: _____

Measurements: _____

_____

Fabrics: _____

_____

_____

Notions: _____

Special notes: _____

_____

Changes to original concept: _____

_____

_____

Date completed: _____

fabric

DATE: _____

SOURCE: _____

YARDAGE: _____

COST: _____

DATE: _____

SOURCE: _____

YARDAGE: _____

COST: _____

DATE: _____

SOURCE: _____

YARDAGE: _____

COST: _____

DATE: _____

SOURCE: _____

YARDAGE: _____

COST: _____

DATE: _____

SOURCE: _____

YARDAGE: _____

COST: _____

DATE: _____

SOURCE: _____

YARDAGE: _____

COST: _____

DATE: _____

SOURCE: _____

YARDAGE: _____

COST: _____

DATE: _____

SOURCE: _____

YARDAGE: _____

COST: _____

Gifts IN A Jiff

DATE MADE/NEEDED: . . . .

OCCASION:. . . . .

FOR WHOM:. . . . .

PROJECT DESCRIPTION:. . . . .

. . . .

MATERIALS: . . . .

. . . .

COST PER GIFT: . . . .

Triumphs

	COMPLETED DATE
1.	
2.	
3.	
4.	
5.	

. . . .

Conquer

	GOAL DATE
1.	
2.	
3.	
4.	
5.	

Playsuits from Old Dresses

Several years ago I unwittingly got into a small money-making plan. I had quite a few summer dresses that I was tired of but that were still too good to discard, so I decided to remake them into play suits to wear in the garden. I measured down from the waist to where my shorts would ordinarily extend, then cut off all around the dress, allowing for a small hem. In the center of the front and back of the dress, I cut a slash 6" long. From the cutoff bottom piece, I cut out two triangular pieces and sewed one into the slash in front and one in back and put in snaps. It makes a very pretty and quick transformation from tired old dress to perky playsuit. I have been doing this for my friends and neighbors for $1.50 per dress ever since. It's so simple, and you don't seem to mind wearing your old dresses again.

— Mrs. John Schmidt

From "Women Who Make Cents"
July 1955 issue of *The* WORKBASKET

151

THE ART OF EMBROIDERY

All stitches are started on the wrong side of the material by making two or three small stitches, one over the other, to anchor the thread. Never make a knot.

✳ Outline or Stem Stitch—This stitch is worked from left to right. Bring the needle up through the fabric to the right side on the line to be outlined. Holding the thread toward you as shown (or the thread may be swung to the left away from you), take a short slanting backstitch along the stamped line. Make the next and each successive stitch from right to left and bring the needle out to the left at the end of the previous stitch. Repeat along the line, keeping the stitches small and uniform.

✳ Whipped Stem Stitch—Outline the design in an outline stitch; then, in contrasting thread, whipstitch over the stem stitch.

✳ Running Stitch—This stitch is used for outline and padding. The needle is carried in and out of the material, making small up-and-down, even stitches. Take several stitches on the needle before drawing it through.

✳ Threaded Running Stitch—Outline the design in a running stitch, then weave a thread in and out of the running stitch. A contrasting thread may be used if desired.

Outline or Stem Stitch

Whipped Stem Stitch

Running Stitch

Threaded Running Stitch

Whipped Running Stitch

Chainstitch

Backstitch

Threaded Backstitch

❊ Whipped Running Stitch—Outline the design in a running stitch, then whipstitch over the running stitch.

❊ Chainstitch—Bring the thread to the right side of the material, hold the thread toward you with your left thumb, take a stitch into the same hole where the thread was brought up, forming a small loop. Do not pull the thread tightly. Bring the needle out a short distance forward and over the loop. Make a second loop overlapping the first one. Continue along the marked line.

❊ Backstitch—Take a small running stitch, insert the needle at the end of the running stitch, thrust the needle through to the wrong side and over twice as much space as the original stitch on the wrong side; bring the needle to the right side and repeat.

❊ Threaded Backstitch—Outline the design in a simple backstitch, then weave in and out with one or two contrasting threads.

Embroidery continued on page 154»

✻ Crossed Backstitch—On the right side, this stitch resemble two rows of backstitch, and on the wrong side, the catchstitch. Slant the needle the same as if making a catchstitch, make a single backstitch, first on the lower side and then diagonally across on the upper side. Work this stitch on transparent material so the crossing of threads shows through to the right side. This stitch is often called the herringbone stitch when the crosses are worked on the right side.

✻ Cross-Stitch—Crosses are stamped on the material, or a design may be worked on the material of a uniform weave like monk's cloth or on checked gingham. Make a slanting stitch from the lower left to the upper right corner of the cross. Make a second slanting stitch from the lower right to the upper left corner of the cross. All crosses should be worked the same way to give a uniform appearance to the work. In working long rows with the same color, all stitches slanting in one direction may be made across the row, then worked back, crossing all stitches in the other direction.

✻ Double Overcasting—With a heavy corded embroidery thread, overcast the turned hem edge with even, slanting stitches ¼" deep. Finish the edge, turn the fabric, and work a second row, matching the stitches at each end.

February 1953

Crossed Backstitch
(Right Side)

Crossed Backstitch (Wrong Side)

Cross-Stitch

Double Overcasting

Needle Pointers

FROM OCTOBER 1951
AND MARCH 1950

* If you're not sure how to cut part of your pattern and no help is available, try cutting that part out of muslin or any spare piece of fabric you have.

* Use a long stitch and loose tension to sew jersey fabrics— similar to that used when machine basting.

* Dress up a plain blouse or dress by carrying an extra set of buttons, such as rhinestone buttons sewn on small pieces that snap onto the blouse or dress.

* Always buy more material than the pattern calls for when making a plaid dress or blouse. It is most important that the plaid should be matched at the seams. Choose a simple pattern with little or no detail. It is smart to cut each piece single and match the plaid perfectly.

* Skirts often sag or hang crooked because they are not cut with the grain of fabric as directed.

* Pressing as you sew is essential for a more professional look. Press darts before they are sewn in a seam. If the darts are large,

slash through the center and press open.

* Bear in mind the weight of fabric you will be working with when selecting the size of your needle. It should always be a little thicker than the thread so it goes into the material easily.

* Every sewing basket should have at least two pairs of scissors; one large pair for cutting out fabric and a small pair to cut thread.

* Before attempting to cut a garment, press all pattern pieces and material if necessary. Cut out on a smooth flat surface; mark all perforations and cut notches out from seams.

* Pile fabrics, such as velvet and corduroy, should be cut with the pile and design going up. This is sometimes difficult, but be sure all pieces are cut in the same direction.

* An emery board and a pair of eyebrow tweezers are handy to have around the sewing machine. They are wonderful for smoothing the surface of a pin or needle pulling short threads.

Favorite Sources

Fabric, Notions, Thread, Sewing Machine Brand and Repair, both online and local.

NAME: _____

ADDRESS: _____

PHONE: _____

E-MAIL: _____

WEBSITE: _____

NOTES: _____

_____

NAME: _____

ADDRESS: _____

PHONE: _____

E-MAIL: _____

WEBSITE: _____

NOTES: _____

_____

NAME: _____

ADDRESS: _____

PHONE: _____

E-MAIL: _____

WEBSITE: _____

NOTES: _____

_____

NAME: _____

ADDRESS: _____

PHONE: _____

E-MAIL: _____

WEBSITE: _____

NOTES: _____

_____

NAME: _____

ADDRESS: _____

PHONE: _____

E-MAIL: _____

WEBSITE: _____

NOTES: _____

_____

NAME: _____

ADDRESS: _____

PHONE: _____

E-MAIL: _____

WEBSITE: _____

NOTES: _____

_____

INDEX

The WORKBASKET Sewing Workbook. Copyright © 2011 by F+W Media, Inc. Manufactured in China. All rights reserved. No part of this book may be reproduced in any form or by any electronic or mechanical means including information storage and retrieval systems without permission in writing from the publisher, except by a reviewer who may quote brief passages in a review. Published by Krause Publications, a division of F+W Media, Inc., 10150 Carver Rd, Blue Ash, OH 45242. (800) 289-0963. First Edition.

15   14   13   12   11   5   4   3   2   1

DISTRIBUTED IN CANADA BY FRASER DIRECT
100 Armstrong Avenue
Georgetown, ON, Canada L7G 5S4
Tel: (905) 877-4411

DISTRIBUTED IN THE U.K. AND EUROPE BY F&W MEDIA INTERNATIONAL
Brunel House, Newton Abbot, Devon, TQ12 4PU, England
Tel: (+44) 1626 323200, Fax: (+44) 1626 323319
E-mail: enquiries@fwmedia.com

DISTRIBUTED IN AUSTRALIA BY CAPRICORN LINK
P.O. Box 704, S. Windsor NSW, 2756 Australia
Tel: (02) 4577-3555

SRN: W6539
ISBN-10: 1-4402-2870-1
ISBN-13: 978-1-4402-2870-4

Edited by *Bethany Anderson*

Designed by *Julie Barnett*

Production coordinated by *Greg Nock*

Illustrations from *The WORKBASKET*

www.fwmedia.com

METRIC CONVERSION CHART

to convert	to	multiply by
inches	centimeters	2.54
centimeters	inches	0.4
feet	centimeters	30.5
centimeters	feet	0.03
yards	meters	0.9
meters	yards	1.1